70Candles! Gatherings
A Leader's Guide

by

Jane Giddan and Ellen Cole

Cult Classics Publisher

Carrollton, Texas

USA

70Candles! Gatherings

A Leader's Guide

ISBN 10: 0-9981068-1-X

ISBN 13: 978-0-9981068-1-6

70Candles! Gatherings

A Leader's Guide

by

Jane Giddan and Ellen Cole

INTRODUCTION

Welcome to 70Candles!

This guide answers requests made on our 70candles.com blog. Women near and in their 70's have asked for opportunities to discuss, with their age-mates, issues important to them. This booklet will help you create, host, and facilitate 70Candles! Gatherings in your geographic area.

Our book, *70Candles! Women Thriving in Their 8th Decade*, published by the Taos Institute, identifies and discusses themes and topics that we've found matter most to women our age in this unique era of extended longevity. These topics are wonderful catalysts for rich discussion.

We've discovered how much women enjoy talking with each other about common-held issues—joys and challenges—and we've seen how important other women are to a sense of well-being as we age. In the pages that follow you will find guidelines and suggestions for conducting a "somewhat organized" gathering. These ideas will be useful, whether you meet just once or continue on a regular basis over time. We hope you find the conversations as lively and heartfelt, poignant and inspiring, as we have. Be ready to laugh a lot and perhaps shed a few tears, all in the company of your age-mates.

CREATING A GROUP

GATHERING PARTICIPANTS

Aim for a group of 10-15 women, but it's reasonable to consider a smaller number at first, with room to grow. To find them:

- Communicate on the 70Candles! Gatherings page of the 70candles.com blog.

- Invite your own friends and acquaintances, through phone calls, email, Facebook, and other social media.

   (See Appendix A for a sample announcement/invitation)

- Post information at your community Senior Center or Recreation Center.

- Submit information to your community newspaper.

- Have women bring friends.

- Have women RSVP with their email address so you know how to contact them and how many participants to expect.

- Set a time limit for the first meeting. Two-hours works well.

- Determine at the end if there's interest (real interest) in the group continuing. If so, future meetings could be monthly.

THE SETTING

- If in a home, arrange for comfortable seating, preferably in more or less a circle, where women can see each other.

- If at a restaurant, a church, or another public space, a round table in a separate quiet room works best.

- Offer snacks and drinks upon arrival, while participants fill out informational index cards and greet each other.

SUPPLIES

- Name tags, with large print, are optional, but very helpful.

- Index cards for (a) contact information, (b) demographics that you'd like to know, such as age, work status, type of residence (e.g., private home, apartment, senior living), marital/partner status, and (c) anything a participant wants to be sure gets discussed.

- Several pads of lined paper and pens for notetaking during the break-out sessions.

- Printed question sheets for selected break-out topics; one for each small group (See appendix C). These are especially useful for encouraging participation in the initial session. However, if the gathering is small, it might be easier to have the group as a whole stay together to focus on selected topics.

ROLE OF THE FACILITATOR

- Have in mind a rough schedule for the gathering, and be sure to keep an eye on the clock.

- Begin with introductions, including your own (details below).

- Acknowledge each contribution from participants to encourage deeper sharing and conversation. This might include nodding your head, expressing thanks, or rephrasing the comment. You may offer any facts or ask questions that seem relevant.

- Allow for responses and extended conversation.

- Offer pertinent facts and ask relevant questions.

- Be sure everyone has a chance to participate. This might include interrupting or gently confronting a participant who begins to dominate the conversation. Or it might include directly asking a quiet member a question.

- Summarize and move on to the next topic.

This outline provides an overview of a typical gathering. More details are offered in the pages ahead.

DISCUSSION FORMAT-OUTLINE

1. Determine the length of the meeting.

2. Select a record keeper.

3. Provide amplification, if needed.

4. Begin with introductions.

5. Present Longevity Facts and related historical information, described below.

6. Divide participants into small brainstorming groups of 3-4 women.

7. Return to the group as a whole for collaborative discussion on all the small group topics.

8. Summarize and present what newer research tells us is the good news about life at this age.

9. End with a portion of the poem in Appendix D, perhaps the first and final two stanzas.

10. Discuss future plans for the group.

DISCUSSION FORMAT

1. Length of meeting - A 2-hour block of time allows for initial greetings, snacks, the group discussion, and planning for the future.

2. Record keeping - It is very helpful to have someone in the group take notes to record important topics raised. These notes can be edited and sent out to participants, and they are extremely useful for planning future gatherings.

3. Amplification - A simple microphone with 20-foot cord and small portable amplifier may be useful, and appreciated, if available.

4. Introductions - Have each participant say her name and one thing she'd like the group to know about herself.

For future meetings:

- Say something for which you are grateful
- Share one new thing you did this week
- Describe one kindness you bestowed
- Tell about one kindness you received

The group leader can then share a brief bio about herself and why she offered to convene this group.

5. Present the following Longevity Facts and related historical information.

LONGEVITY FACTS

We are survivors!
We're in the vanguard of the longevity revolution.
Over the last century, we gained on average, 30 years of life span.

Average life expectancy
For most of human evolution – 19 to 20 years
For the Romans - 27 years
In 1800 - 35 years
In 1900 - 47 years

Then, because of improved sanitation, public health, immunizations, antibiotics, sterilization, safer childbirth, etc.
In 2000 - 78 years

Today—Women's average life expectancy in the US is 81.2 years…five years longer than men!

Nowadays, if you've reached 65, you're expected to live to 85 or beyond.

The fastest growing part of our population is people over 85

One of four 65-year-olds today will live past 90

One of ten 65-year-olds today will live past 95

There has been a reversal in the age pyramid.
Now, there are more grandparents than grandchildren.
By the time our grandchildren reach old age, living to 100 will be commonplace.

More than half those born since 2000 are expected to live to 100!
The good news is we are living longer and healthier.

The question for you is: How to use this gift of time?

The goal of those who study positive aging is this: To add not just more years to our lives, but more life to our years (George Vaillant).

And food for thought: How might we be advocates for the positive side of aging? How might we counter ageism and our society's bias against signs of aging and the aged?

See if you can find some answers as you discuss topics from the book, 70Candles! Women Thriving in Their 8th Decade by Jane Giddan and Ellen Cole.

This discussion group is part of a new national "movement," as 70Candles! Gatherings are emerging across the country and beyond.

THE HISTORY OF THE 70CANDLES! PROJECT

The Authors
(See more complete bios in Appendix B)

Jane Giddan & Ellen Cole, BFF's since 9th grade, grew up in New York City. They stayed in touch through the decades as they graduated, pursued careers, married, had children and moved around the country.

Then in the year 2000, as they neared their 70th birthdays, Ellen visited Jane in Dallas, Texas, and they compared notes. They were both making major transitions in their lives.

They had in common moves to a new location: Ellen and her husband from Anchorage, Alaska to Albany, New York; Jane and her husband from Toledo, Ohio to Dallas, Texas.

Both were leaving old pals behind and having to make new friends.

There were major shifts in their careers.

Both moved closer to family.

They wondered about what it meant to be 70 or more.
They knew they were not like their grandmothers at this age.
They were curious about what they might experience in the decade ahead.

Readings

Academics that they were, they first looked to published literature, but were dismayed at what they found. Lots of research in medicine, psychology, sociology, and gerontology focused on the downside of aging. They dubbed the research "Sick Granny Studies." Little was targeted to healthy women in their 70's.

About this time, Ellen, who already had a PhD, decided to pursue a second Master of Arts degree, this time in Applied Positive Psychology (MAPP) at the University of Pennsylvania; a program started by noted psychologist Martin Seligman.

A main tenet of Positive Psychology is "PERMA"— an acronym for the components of life satisfaction:

P-Positive emotions

E-Engagement (sometimes called "flow")

R-Relationships

M-Meaning

A-Accomplishments

Ellen decided to do her culminating paper (her "Capstone Project") on positive aging, and it was a natural for Ellen and Jane to join forces to collect data. Little did they know at the time, but their main finding turned out to be the power and the satisfaction of gathering together with age-mates. This project turned out for both to be a picture-perfect example of PERMA in action.

The Blog

- They decided to start an on-line blog, to ask real women what was up.

  They called it 70candles.com — Who has seen it?

- They wanted to know what it was like to be a woman in her 70's today.

- They asked women to share joys and challenges.

- Were they still working for a paycheck?

- How can we flourish as we proceed through this decade?

- Lo and behold, women began speaking to each other on that blog; women from around the world sharing ideas and offering support, from South Africa, to London, Australia, Israel, and across the United States

- The 70candles.com blog continues to this day, stronger than ever, with new heartwarming, and sometimes heartbreaking, entries each week. Women who elect to become email subscribers to the site receive an email notice of each new posting.

Gatherings

Then they thought...why not gather women together in a room to speak to each other face-to-face?

And so began the 70Candles! Gatherings.

They assembled eight groups in the first year...82 voices across the country:

One group in Philadelphia, Pennsylvania, two in New York City, two in Albany, New York, one in Ithaca New York, and two in Dallas, Texas.

These are the questions they posed to the discussion groups:

1) What was or is the meaning of work in your life? How does your idea of yourself (your identity) change when you cease to practice your profession/job?

2) How do you deal with/think about loss of function (memory, hearing, vision, balance, ability to multi-task, etc.)?

3) How do you think others see you? How does it feel to be the oldest person in the room?

4) What is life like for you today? What are your challenges? What are your joys? When do you feel at your best? What contributes to your well-being?

5) What advice would you give to younger women, perhaps to the baby boomers close on our heels, to prepare for turning 70?

6) What do you know now that you wish you had known then?

7) What do you wish you had done differently?

8) Is there anything you wish you had learned or accomplished that you can't do now?

9) Summary Question: What does it take to thrive in this, our eighth decade?

More recently, through the 70candles.com blog's 70Candles! Gatherings Page, new discussion groups began to form in many more cities and towns.

Huffington Post

The Huffington Post then invited Jane and Ellen to blog at Huff/Post50. The columns they have written can be found at:

Huffingtonpost.com/jane-giddan-and-ellen-cole

The Book

What they learned through their explorations is summarized in *70Candles! Women Thriving in Their 8th Decade.*

Their book was published in the summer of 2015 by Taos Institute Publications, purveyors of the excellent on-line Positive Aging Newsletter.

It is available at *Taosinstitute.net/70candles* and at *Amazon.com* in paperback and as a Kindle and Nook download.

Their Findings

From all their sources, they distilled the Concerns of Women in Their 70's.

Realizing that there might still be decades of life ahead for them, these women assessed their world at this stage and examined their options.

Here are the topics that mattered most to them:

- **Work and Retirement:** When is the right time, if ever, to retire? What to do with the ocean of unstructured time that lies beyond many long and frequently satisfying careers? How to stay engaged, feel fulfilled, and participate meaningfully?

- **Living Arrangements:** Where to live once the family home becomes a burden? Stay in place? Move near family? Remain in familiar terrain, but smaller quarters? Become involved in a new community? Mobility in any community is always an issue.

- **Ageism:** How to react to the attitudes of others...even old people who view old age with pessimism, curiosity, fear, even disdain? Our hope was, and is, to create a legion of anti-ageism activists, with the impact of those in the women's movement that began when we were young adults in the 1960's and 1970's.

- **Caretaking:** Many are taking care of parents, partners or spouses, and even grandchildren, and feel the stress—as well as the satisfaction—of that responsibility.

- Social Connections: Above all, they do not want to be isolated, but seek social connections. They take courses, volunteer their time, continue in their long-established careers, participate in local activities, and travel with others. They feel especially grateful for the support from their women age-mates and friends.

- Functional Changes: Although these women acknowledge bodily changes, they try to go forth, regardless. They stay active and avail themselves of the newest technology—hearing aids, stylish eyeglasses, new hips, mobility scooters.

- Grandparenting: There are so many ways to be a grandparent, especially when families are spread across the country. Some feel estranged and disconnected, while others derive joy from frequent Skype-ing and periodic visits. Still others play an integral, everyday role and may wonder if it's too much.

- Our Relationship to Technology: Is it possible to keep up?

  - Computer natives—the toddlers of today
  - Computer immigrants—our children
  - Computer refugees—our generation

- Loss and the End of Life: How to face the loss of dear friends and family members, and deal with unavoidable sadness and grief. And ultimately, how to prepare for the end of one's own life.

There was no single answer to any of these.

They are issues we all think about and continue to explore.

Here's a chance for you to share your views.

6. At this point, divide participants into small discussion groups as follows:

BREAK-OUT GROUPS

3-4 women in a group works well.

Give each group a printed sheet with a different topic to ponder, along with a pen and pad of paper.

Have a scribe in each group take notes.

After 15-20 minutes, return to the group as a whole.

Following are questions that can stimulate rich conversation in the break-out groups.

(See Appendix C for suggested page layout)

The number of questions used at any meeting will vary with the number of participants, and the size of the small groups.

1) WHAT ARE YOUR THOUGHTS ABOUT THE TRANSITION FROM WORK LIFE TO RETIREMENT?

2) WHAT DO YOU THINK ABOUT WHERE AND HOW YOU MIGHT LIVE IN YOUR UPCOMING YEARS?

3) HOW DO YOU THINK YOU MIGHT RESPOND TO THE TRANSITION IF/WHEN YOU CHANGE YOUR PLACE OF RESIDENCE? HOW MIGHT YOUR SOCIAL LIFE/RELATIONSHIPS BE AFFECTED?

4) WHAT CONTRIBUTES TO YOUR WELL-BEING AT THIS STAGE OF LIFE?

5) WHAT NEEDS TO CHANGE IN OUR COMMUNITIES AND IN OUR SOCIETY TO ACCOMMODATE OUR AGING POPULATION?

6) WHAT DOES THE PHRASE "GIFT OF TIME" MEAN TO YOU? DOES THINKING ABOUT IT MAKE YOU WANT TO CHANGE ANYTHING IN YOUR LIFE RIGHT NOW?

7) FUNCTIONAL CHANGES (HEARING, EYESIGHT, STRENGTH, VARIOUS SURGERIES RELATED TO AGE) ARE INEVITABLE. HOW HAVE YOU AND YOUR BODY RESPONDED SO FAR?

8) WHAT ARE YOUR ROLES IF SANDWICHED BETWEEN YOUNGER AND OLDER GENERATIONS (SOMETIMES CALLED THE "CLUB SANDWICH GENERATION")?

9) WHAT IS YOUR RELATIONSHIP TO TECHNOLOGY? DO YOU FEEL AS THOUGH YOU'VE "KEPT UP?

10) WHAT IS YOUR BEST ADVICE ABOUT FINANCES FOR ANYONE EXPECTING TO GET OLD?

11) WHAT DO YOU WISH YOU HAD DONE DIFFERENTLY, AND WHAT DO YOU WISH YOU WOULD HAVE KNOWN WHEN YOU WERE YOUNGER?

12) WHAT HAS BEEN YOUR EXPERIENCE WITH LOSS OF FAMIY MEMBERS AND FRIENDS?

13) WHAT DOES IT TAKE TO THRIVE AND FLOURISH IN THIS DECADE OF YOUR LIFE?

7. Return to the group as a whole.

Have a spokesperson from each small group summarize the results of that group's conversation. Allow responses and widen the discussion, so the larger group has opportunities to add/respond to each topic in turn. This conversation, then, really becomes the heart of the gathering.

Moderate and follow the flow of the interactions.

8. Summarize and present what newer research tells us is the good news about life at this age.

THE GOOD NEWS! Findings from newer research

"Social ties reduce the risk of disease by lowering blood pressure, heart rate and cholesterol." "Friends are helping us live longer" (Nurses Health Study, Harvard Medical School ref Taylor and Klein, 2000).

Social isolation is as big a risk factor for ill health as smoking.

"Successfully aging older adults can be a great resource for younger generations" (Jeste study).

"Empathy—the ability to understand the emotional point of view of another—improves with age" (Gary Small, brain researcher).

"People actually enjoy greater well-being as they age."...even with poor physical health.

Factors that contribute to well-being are psychological: including resilience and absence of depression (Jeste study).

From Laura Carstensen:

New learning seems to change the brain and improve resiliency.

Older people are more likely to focus on the positive when making decisions.

They have fewer arguments and find better solutions to problems.

They are better at controlling emotions and accepting misfortune.

Older people grow better at living in the present. They focus more on things that matter, like feelings and less on long–term goals.

From Martin Seligman:

Personality, social, and cognitive characteristics are relatively stable through adulthood and old age.

Intimate relationships affect how we age. Older adults have higher levels of marital satisfaction.

Aging is a time of freedom, a time to choose to remain busy, productive, and creative...a time to be self-compassionate.

Gratitude, and resilience in the face of adversity, are key factors in life satisfaction and aging well.

9. Conclude by reading aloud from the poem, "At Seventy."

For an initial gathering, recite the first and the last two stanzas of the poem.

(See Appendix D)

10. Discuss future plans for the group.

- See if women want to meet again
- How often to meet
- Where to hold gatherings
- Topics for the next session
- Possible readings
- Choose volunteers to:
  - Make an email list to share
  - Rotate homes or find a suitable location
  - Provide food and drink
  - Take notes

APPENDICIES

APPENDIX A - Invitation

A 70Candles! Gathering

Join a gathering and interactive discussion especially for women our age about the joys and challenges of this time in our lives.

[Leader's name and town], will convene this area's first

70Candles! Gathering inspired by the web blog at 70candles.com

and the book, *70Candles! Women Thriving in Their 8th Decade,*

by Jane Giddan and Ellen Cole.

You are invited for two hours of

good-hearted observations and sharing.

We will meet at

[date, time and location]

Refreshments will be served.

Space is limited.

Please respond to

[Leader's email address]

Appendix B – Expanded Author Bios

Jane Giddan and Ellen Cole became BFF's in 9th grade in New York City. The 1950's were years of their high school adventures, and The City was their playground.

During the 1950's and early 1960's when they were at college (the Eisenhower years) they were part of what was called "the silent generation." When they traveled in Europe during the summer of 1960, they and the world seemed carefree.

Remember, John F. Kennedy was in office from January 1961 to November 22, 1963.

They graduated from college in 1962, Jane from Cornel University, Ellen from Boston University, then went on to graduate school, Jane to Stanford and Ellen to Harvard and later the Union Institute.

Political turmoil began as they finished graduate school…the world was changing. They witnessed the Vietnam War and the assassinations of John F. Kennedy, Martin Luther King, Jr., and Robert Kennedy.

In the mid-to-late 1960's and the early 1970's, they both married, had children, and began their careers for real.

Ellen became a counseling psychologist and an academic, focusing on women, gender, and human sexuality. Jane became a speech-language pathologist, and a professor in a department of psychiatry, specializing in autism and communication disorders in child mental health.

In their early married years, they and their peers marched for civil rights, against the Vietnam War, and for the rights of women in the second wave of the Women's Movement. They were advocates for "women's liberation." They met with other women in encounter groups to explore new possibilities. During the 1980's to 2000 they pursued careers, followed spouses across the country, and always stayed in touch with each other.

Then in the year 2000, as they neared their 70th birthdays, Ellen visited Jane in Dallas, Texas, and they compared notes. They were both making major transitions in their lives.

They had in common moves to a new location: Ellen with her husband from Anchorage, Alaska to Albany, New York and Jane with her husband from Toledo, Ohio to Dallas, Texas.

Both were leaving old friends behind and having to make new ones. There were major shifts in their careers. Both moved closer to family. They wondered about what it meant to be nearly 70, for they knew they were not like their grandmothers at this age. They were curious about what they might experience in the decade ahead.

Appendix C - Break-out group printed question format

This is a useful way to lay out the question pages for small-group discussions. Group responses can be written here and on pads of paper provided.

70Candles! Women Thriving in Their 8th Decade

GROUP DISCUSSION

TOPIC: **WHAT DO YOU THINK ABOUT WHERE AND HOW YOU MIGHT LIVE IN YOUR UPCOMING YEARS?**

OPTIONS   CHALLENGES   JOYS

ADVICE TO YOUNGER GENERATIONS

Appendix D - POEM   At Seventy by Caroline M. Simon © 2014

At seventy backs ache, knees creak, minds wander and smiles broaden.
Parts that used to take care of themselves need tending.
And even though we don't want to believe it,
We are much further from the beginning than we are from the ending.

At seventy our children are grown up people
With jobs, lives, joys and troubles of their own.
Our grandchildren grow taller and smarter as we shrink and stretch.
And we all travel to places so far away
Our postcards take two weeks to deliver.
We smile as the kids tell us of their work, which we don't understand,
Of their friends, whose names we can't pronounce properly,
And of their aspirations which make us swell with pride and smile with memory.

At seventy we've grown up, but have not finished learning.
We seek simplicity and quiet joy
A walk through the park with a child in hand,
A stroll through a market in a foreign land,
Celebrations with family and friends,
A happy meeting of means and ends.
We pray for favorable test results, everyone's good health and a winning hand,
And just once in a while something going according to plan.
As we balance those we've lost with those we've gained.

At seventy, we forget where we put our keys,
Our cars and our appointment books.
But we know by heart how to fit the pieces of life together,
How to make lemonade out of lemons
And interesting patchwork patterns out of torn pieces of cloth.

At seventy our friends say we look "young and thin" before their cataract surgery,
Our grandchildren tell us we are "old and round" before they learn to lie,
And we still seek engagement with a world that doesn't much care what we are doing.

At seventy we can enjoy a good book, if we can find our glasses;
A good meal with our friends, if we eat early enough;
A beautiful place with those we love, if we stay out of the sun;
And our own company.

At seventy precautions are second nature.
Social Security and Medicare are old friends.
What we want of ourselves and others seems possible,
And love, laughter and time are far more precious than jewels.

At seventy,
Injustice still rankles,
Empathy heightens,
Experience matters.
And loving kindness counts the most,
At seventy.

RECOMMENDED READING

Brody, J. (2009). *Jane Brody's guide to the great beyond: A practical primer to help you and your loved ones prepare medically, legally and emotionally for the end of life.* New York: Random House.

Buettner, D. (2012). *The Blue Zones, Second edition: 9 lessons for living longer from the people who've lived the longest.* Washington DC: National Geographic.

Carstensen, L. L. (2009). *A long bright future: An action plan for a lifetime of happiness, health, and financial security.* New York: Broadway Books.

Cole, E. & Gergen, M. (eds.). (2012). *Retiring but not shy: Feminist psychologists create their post-careers.* Chagrin Falls, OH: Taos Institute Publications.

Friedman, D. A. (2015). *Jewish wisdom for growing older: Finding your grit and grace beyond midlife.* Woodstock, VT: Jewish Lights Publishing.

Gawande, A. (2014). *Being mortal: Medicine and what matters in the end.* New York: Metropolitan Books.

Giddan, J. & Cole, E. (2015). *70Candles! Women thriving in their 8th decade.* Chagrin Falls, OH: Taos Institute Publications.

Jeste, D. (2005). "Secrets of Successful Aging: An Expert Interview with Dilip Jeste, MD." *Medscape.com.*

Pillemer, K. (2011). *30 lessons for living: Tried and true advice from the wisest Americans.* New York: Hudson Street Press.

Pogrebin, L. C. (2013). *How to be a friend to a friend who's sick.* New York: Public Affairs.

Reivich, K., & Shatte, A. (2002). *The resilience factor: 7 keys to finding your inner strength and overcoming life's hurdles.* New York: Broadway Books.

ACKNOWLEDGMENTS

We appreciate the thoughtful feedback from Cynthia Carlburg, Evelyn Eskin, Lisa Fromm-Sarto, Gabrielle Giddan, Karen Lovelace, and Sandra Peck, who were readers of early versions of this Guide. Their many ideas have made this booklet clearer and easier to use.

Our many thanks to Caroline M. Simon for permission to include her wonderful poem, "At Seventy."

NOTES

NOTES